How to Be Sexy

Carmen Electra

WITH SHERYL BERK

BROADWAY BOOKS * NEW YORK

PUBLISHED BY BROADWAY BOOKS

Published in the United States by Broadway Books, an imprint of The Doubleday
Broadway Publishing Group, a division of Random House, Inc., New York.
www.broadwaybooks.com

BROADWAY BOOKS and its logo, a letter B bisected on the diagonal, are trademarks
of Random House, Inc.

All photographs © by Michael Simon and Albert Ferreira
Book design by Caroline Cunningham

No book can replace the diagnostic expertise and medical advice of a trusted physician. Please be
certain to consult with your doctor before making any decisions that affect your health, particularly
if you suffer from any medical condition or have any symptom that may require treatment.

Library of Congress Cataloging-in-Publication Data
Electra, Carmen.
    How to be sexy / Carmen Electra with Sheryl Berk. — 1st ed.
        p.   cm.
    (alk. paper)
    1. Women—Psychology.   2. Sexual attraction.   3. Beauty, Personal.   4. Femininity.
    5. Women—Conduct of life.   I. Berk, Sheryl.   II. Title.
    HQ1206.E445   2006
    646.7'042—dc22   2007001356

ISBN: 978-0-7679-2541-9

PRINTED IN THE UNITED STATES OF AMERICA

10 9 8 7 6 5 4 3 2 1

First Edition

For my mom, Patricia Rose Kincade, who taught me what it is to be a strong, sexy woman, and for my sister, Debbi

CONTENTS

How to Be Sexy

CHAPTER 1

What Is Sexy?

There's a saying basketball coaches are fond of: "You can't teach height." I think a lot of people consider sex appeal an attribute like height—you've either got it or you don't. Well, let me let you in on a little secret—you can learn to be sexy. I know what you're thinking, "No, Carmen, *you* can learn to be sexy, *I* can learn how to knit. I don't have *that* kind of body, or *that* kind of attitude, or *that* kind of confidence. I just don't have what it takes, period." I'm here to tell you that you just don't have it *yet*.

I'll be honest with you: I was always boy crazy. I had a boyfriend in kindergarten. Rod Stewart's "Do Ya Think I'm Sexy?" was my theme song when I was younger, and I wore tight jeans to school (my poor mom!). But even with this innate sexy sixth sense, I didn't always get it right—or know what to do with it. Over the years, I was constantly experimenting with new looks, trying to maximize my sex appeal. Learning how to harness your sexuality takes time and maturity. Sexiness gives you a sense of power and control—if you're sexy, people are drawn to you like bees to honey. I had to learn to work my best assets (and occasionally shake 'em) to get where I am today (and it paid off—if I didn't feel sexy, I wouldn't have a job!), and now I'd like to share what I've learned with you.

What can you expect in this book? There will be a lot of tips, techniques, and anecdotes culled from my adventures in modeling, acting, dancing, dating, mating, and beyond. I like to think I've learned a thing or two along the way. I also have been really lucky to work with some of the most amazing people in Hollywood: the stylists, makeup artists, trainers, and coaches who could turn anyone—even dowdy Queen Elizabeth—into a bombshell, and I've called on their expertise as well.

The first lesson you need to learn is that you are your own "sexpert." Sexy is personal—everyone has her own way of seeing it, and most important, being it. What's sexy for one person may not be sexy for someone else. And your own feelings on sexiness can change from year to year, week to week, day to day.

Take me, for example. I think lots of things are sexy. Black leather and handcuffs? Totally sexy. Tattoos and piercings? Definitely. But I also think being with a trustworthy and loving person who takes care of you is sexy. I think holding hands is sexy, but so is a guy who can dominate or likes it when I do. A low-cut gown and mile-high stilettos? Hot! Jeans, a tank top, and a pair of Chucks? Ditto.

Okay, Carmen, you say, how are you going to help me be sexy if you can't give me any hard and fast rules?

Well, that's just the thing—there are none. What I can tell you is how and where to start your own personal journey to sexiness. To find your own sexy self, you need to be comfortable and confident with the person you are. You have to like the lady you see in the mirror—truly like her, inside and out. I know that's not always easy.

Believe me, there are days when I don't feel pretty or poised; when I doubt myself and am insecure and nervous and would much rather stay in bed all day than get up and do an interview or walk a red carpet. Any woman who tells you she doesn't feel that way at least once in a while is lying; we're all human. Everyone has a bad hair day or wakes up feeling bloated or wishes she was just ten pounds thinner or two inches taller or five years younger. And I guarantee that whenever I feel that way, whenever my confidence starts to slip, it shows . . . big time.

So that's where it all begins: with an inner confidence that radiates outward. Once you have that, you can share it with the world through what you wear, how you style your hair and makeup, how you carry yourself (and the later chapters in my book will help you do all that with expert advice from the people who help me look great). All of those things are easy to figure out; it's the inner work that really takes time and effort and dedication. You have to do your homework and a whole lot of soul searching to discover the real you. And at first, the person you find might come as a total shock or surprise—she might be very different from the girl you were growing up or the image your friends and family have of you. You don't have to please anybody but yourself or live up to anyone else's expectations. That itself is another key to being sexy. You need to be secure enough to not care (too much) what people think.

I'm not saying you shouldn't solicit opinions, I always do. Listen to what people tell you, then make your mind up yourself, staying true to what you believe is right for you. There were countless times I asked my ex-husband, Dave, for his opinion on what outfit I should wear to an event. I'd hold up my favorite and he would say, "I'm not crazy about it." But then I'd look in the mirror and go with it anyway. Why? Because I was the one who had to wear it—and I liked the person I was in it. The ultimate veto power is always yours.

I am lucky enough to have figured out what makes me feel sexy most of the time. People often ask me if anyone taught me to be sexy. I had a lot of great role models who have inspired me and empowered me—many of them from the time I was young—and I've studied them carefully. I've

always had a thing for Ann-Margret. To this day, in her sixties, she has this fire about her. She can be sweet and coy and then, *bang!*, completely explosive. When I first encountered her, I was about twelve years old and in a performing arts school where we were doing the musical *Bye Bye Birdie* so I watched her in the movie. I was mesmerized, and I tried to imitate her way of talking, walking, dancing. She has a breathlessness about her—a wild, chaotic energy that says she doesn't give a damn. She could purr like a kitten and then, in the blink of an eye, turn fierce as a tiger. There ain't nothing sexier than a woman who's unpredictable.

I always admire Jimi Hendrix for his bold sexuality. That voice—you connect with him through his music—it touches you, it forces you to feel. My dad plays guitar, and I remember being a kid and him telling me about this guy Jimi who played left-handed. We'd marvel together that he could make those sounds with his guitar. So I'd sit and listen to his records for hours, transported to another place and time.

Then there was how Hendrix performed onstage—passion, sex, charisma, mystery, danger, all rolled into one. He'd make love to his guitar in a way that made you wish he could take you in his arms and play you. Talk about foreplay. Yet, in interviews, he was far from a wildman—he was very shy and humble. I find that juxtaposition incredibly sexy, too.

So how do you know you have what it takes to be sexy? I can promise you one thing: Everyone has it in her somewhere. It's just a case of finding it and unleashing it. For starters, stop doubting yourself. Sexy comes in all shapes, sizes, and guises. Smart is sexy. Curves are sexy. Being a mother is sexy (you've got all this wisdom and experience under your belt and in your bed!). Sexy can whisper; sexy can shout. Sexy can draw a crowd or hypnotize an individual. Sexy is not being afraid of your own needs, desires, and passions. Sexy is letting go of your inhibitions and insecurities. Sexy is being affectionate, kind, and compassionate. Sexy can be single or a couple. Sexy can be happily ever after, or the here and now.

And sexy is striving to be the best person you can be, which you're already doing. I can't make you change the way you think or feel, but I can help you explore your sexiest self. What you do with what you learn . . . that's all up to you.

Love,

Carmen

DATE MOVIE 2006

CHAPTER 2

Confidence

I wasn't always sure of myself. In fact, I was painfully shy as a kid. I'm talking really shy—the kind of shy where I couldn't even get up in front of the class to read a book report. Okay, maybe part of the problem was—and is—I hate having to read books. Even now, I will never read a novel. The only thing I will read is a script or a self-help book. So the very *idea* of standing in front of a room of people and talking about some boring book made me break into a sweat and feel sick to my stomach. What if I blew it? What if I put everyone to sleep? What if I stuttered or stumbled over a word? The fact that I became an actress still blows my mind.

As you've probably guessed, I developed some techniques for dealing with my fears since my whole job now basically consists of me standing in front of people. I've come a long way, and I'm proud of it. The first few times I did live interviews, it was terrifying. I hadn't found my voice, and I really had no idea how the audience was going to respond or how far I could push it, but the more I did it, the better I got at it. Now I'm actually comfortable talking to Leno or Letterman or just about anyone. I love the spontaneity

and the flirting. I almost forget the cameras are rolling, and I just have the conversation. You know what the trick is? I learned that I shouldn't be afraid to be myself, even if it means I mess up royally and make a fool of myself once in a while. I've learned it's sexy to laugh at my mistakes.

THERE'S NOTHING SEXIER than knowing who you are and having the courage to be that person. Sometimes, it means embracing the one thing that makes you uniquely you. Take Cindy Crawford with her mole or Dave Letterman with his gap teeth—can you imagine either of them without those little imperfections that we love?

The biggest impediment to being sexy is fear. When you think about what's sexy, which do you think of, someone who looks perfectly put together but is hunched over and continually checking herself in the mirror and fussing with her outfit or someone who walks into a room and commands a crowd through her magnetic presence—even if she trips on the way in and has ketchup on her dress? The secret is to stop caring what other people are thinking and focus on being you. It's twisted, I know, but as soon as you stop caring, other people take notice.

A great way to develop confidence is to focus on some way in which you shine and then channel that feeling when you're feeling shaky or unsure. Everyone is good at something. Maybe you've got a killer voice. Maybe you tell amazing jokes. Maybe you can mix a martini like nobody's business. Whatever it is, there's something that you do that you can do without an ounce of fear, and you can use that feeling of assuredness to carry you through moments where you're not at the top of your game.

For me, it's dancing. I get lost in the music, and I forget my fear. When I dance, I feel fantastic—free, bold, and completely confident. It's not a magic bullet, of course. If it were, I could have just signed up for extra tap lessons and never worried about my image again.

The whole audition process was still terrifying to me at the beginning of my career. I knew it was something I needed to confront or it would hold me back forever. I didn't actually confront and deal with it until I was living in L.A. It was the early nineties, I was twenty-one years old, and I already

had my deal with Prince's Paisley Park Records, but I was still struggling. I didn't have any money or a car. I was staying with friends, trying not to give up and go home to Cincinnati. My friends kept telling me, "Carmen, you should get into acting—you have a great look." Me? Act? Talk in front of an audience? Are you kidding? They must have wanted me off their couch bad! It brought back all those horrible memories of book report hell. Not a chance.

Even though I decided to give acting a shot, sometimes I was so nervous that I would walk into an audition, panic, and walk out. Then one day, it hit me: Honey, you are screwing up any chance you might have of finding success here in Hollywood, so you better get a grip. Around that time, I got the audition for MTV's *Singled Out*.

Okay, I told myself, this is your chance. Let go of those fears and give it all you've got. So I went in, I let loose the way I do when I'm dancing, which was what that show was all about anyway, and I ended up getting the job. It changed my life. And I don't just mean landing the show and all the exposure that came with it. What really changed was that I had faced what scared me the most, stared it down, and found my inner strength. The anticipation for me was always the fear factor; all those "what-ifs" that float around your head. What if I screw it up? What if I trip or say something really stupid or everyone laughs? But when I got past all those negative thoughts and just let the real me come through, I realized I was not just okay, I was actually pretty good. I figure, you can either spend your whole life worrying about the "what-ifs" or you can live in the moment, in the present tense, and seize the opportunity to be the person you truly want to be. I am a firm believer that no one and nothing can hold you back from reaching your goals . . . except your own inner demons. That goes with everything you do in life: every business meeting, every date with a new guy, every relationship, even every book report.

I'm not saying I landed this one gig and all my anxieties vanished. I mean, I didn't become Miss Confident overnight, and I'm still working on it.

It takes discipline. I did a lot of work on my self-esteem from that day forward. It's a process, and you need to be patient with yourself.

Baywatch was my next big training ground in that department. Someone on *Baywatch*'s staff had seen a segment I did on *Extra* about *Singled Out* and asked me to audition. I wanted it so bad and I was ready to give it my all, even if it meant working seven days a week, twelve hours a day. But there was just one problem: I'm not a good swimmer. At all. A ton of bricks floats better than I do. I grew up with swimming pools in my neighborhood and the lake nearby, but I was lousy at swimming. I always got water up my nose, so I would never go under without pinching my nose. I went into that audition hoping they wouldn't ask me to swim. I know. I know. It was for *Baywatch*, of course they were going to ask me to swim, but a girl can dream, right? And guess what? In like the first five minutes, they handed me the red swimsuit. I instantly worried about two things: 1) Would I lose the job if I held my nose when I jumped in to save someone's life? And 2) Had I shaved my legs that day? My heart was pounding a million beats a minute, but I wanted that job, so I did it; I jumped into this huge tank, willing myself to just tuck my head and blow air out. I made it across the pool without drowning and I got the job. And okay, I had to take swimming lessons before starting and during the filming of the show, but it was an incredible experience for me. And again, I learned something really important: I had it in me to overcome my fears (and I learned how to swim . . . well kind of!).

My Aha! Moment

I admit it. I owe a big one to Oprah. When it came to finding myself—the real person, not the person I was pretending to be—it was one of her shows that changed my life for the better. It was a really interesting time for me. My career had just started to take off with MTV and *Baywatch*. It was everything I could have dreamed of. I was actually at a dinner meeting with the people from MTV when I got a call from my boyfriend's mom. I remember listening to what she was saying, but not *actually* hearing it. She said, "Something's really wrong. You have to come home now." My mom was in the hospital

and she had a brain tumor. I was in total shock and disbelief. You had to know my mom—she was so strong, a third-degree black belt, a really tough woman. And really, really healthy. Her illness just didn't make sense to me or to any of the people who knew and loved her. It was crazy, and I just couldn't accept it as reality.

The only way I could deal with it was not to deal with it. It was as if by pretending Mom was fine, I'd be helping her get better. So I threw myself into my work. I was shooting *Singled Out* on weekends, *Baywatch* Monday through Friday, working seven days a week. I tried to block it out, to block out the pain and fear of losing her. And I threw myself into the party scene. You find ways to get through stuff. I just thought, Oh, if I have fun and go to clubs, it will distract me from thinking about it. When I was alone, I was overwhelmed with sadness about her situation. I knew part of my constant going out to clubs was the fact that I just couldn't be alone. I always had to have people around me.

My mom died about a year later, and I started to notice that my life wasn't going in the direction I wanted it to. I was sick of it and really sad. I felt like I was running away, trying to escape from the reality of life.

I was watching Oprah and Dr. Phil was on her show. He said in order to heal you have to feel. Suddenly, it clicked with me that I hadn't allowed myself to feel what had been going on in my life. I remember I was on the bed and I let it out—all of it. All that pent-up agony and emotion. I just started to sob. Normally, when I thought about my mom, I would try to distract myself, put the thought out of my head. This time—and for several weeks after—I let myself think of her and miss her and grieve. It hurt. It hurt a lot. I felt a lot of guilt—I hated myself for not being with her more when she was sick. I felt selfish. But at least I was finally taking responsibility. I acknowledged that my mom wasn't coming back and let the loneliness wash over me like a wave then slowly recede. I knew I could get past it. I knew that I needed to change my lifestyle and my outlook. That meant working on both the inside and the outside.

I had a fear of being alone. I had a lot of friendships that were toxic and draining. I needed to let go of them and really be okay with being myself.

The more I got in touch with myself and dealt with the things that were going on in my life, the more my outward appearance—as a reflection of how I felt about who I am and what I stood for—changed as well. Back when I was going to clubs a lot, my style was all about showing skin. Now, I don't feel I need to seek that kind of attention anymore. I'd rather wear a

How to Be Sexy

more stylish outfit than a skimpy, outrageous one that leaves nothing to the imagination. Which isn't to say I don't occasionally love to strut around in garters and a bra and panties. The difference is the motivation behind it. Back then I felt like I *had* to do it all the time. I was dressing for attention: I wanted people to notice me and I thought that was the only way they would. Today, I am much more secure and directed in myself. If I want to look sexy now and wear something outrageously provocative, I feel more empowered. I do it for me, not for anyone else's approval. That's what confidence is all about. And to think it took Oprah and Dr. Phil to finally get through to me.

I Think I Can, I Think I Can . . .

So you wanna be cool as a cucumber in any situation? Think the little engine that could. Seriously, for me, it starts with a single, positive thought: I can do this. I'm worthy. I deserve it. I'm here for a reason. And whatever happens, I can walk away knowing I gave it my best shot. I've always been a cheerleader to my friends and people I care about. I think a lot of women do this. They're generous with others—always encouraging their friends and family and seeing the best in them—but they're stingy with themselves. I was my own worst enemy for the longest time—the queen of self-sabotage. I wasn't able to focus on the best things in myself; instead, I'd focus on my flaws. Isn't that ridiculous? I know I've been blessed with a great life and I've been really fortunate with the success that I've had, so why would I focus on my weaknesses? What I know now is that your inner dialogue is really important. For example, if you tell yourself, "I'm gonna suck," there's a really good chance you will. But I really retrained my thought process: "Be yourself, and it will be fine." And it usually is. And positive thinking even has health benefits: I recently read an article in *The New York Times* about scientists who found that optimists live longer.

But I'd be lying if I said I didn't still freak out once in a while. When I met Ben Stiller and Owen Wilson on the audition for *Starsky & Hutch* I almost lost it. Those guys are hilarious—and such huge stars. I'm a big fan of their movies, so I could barely concentrate on my lines, I just kept thinking, Oh my god, I'm doing scenes with *Ben and Owen.* I was lucky because they are so nice and put me at ease quickly, and I remembered that if I just let go of my hang-ups, no one else would care about them either.

Laugh, Even if Your Butt Is Showing

I am always happy when people tell me I have a good sense of humor. I try so hard not to take myself too seriously because it's a recipe for a nervous breakdown. I know I am not perfect, no one is, and if you don't laugh at your mistakes, you'll cry over them. Besides, laughing is incredibly sexy, and

laughing at yourself doubly so because it shows you're not uptight. No wonder a great sense of humor always tops those lists in all the men's mags of what men really find attractive (along with a big pair of boobs, of course). I have had some pretty embarrassing moments that could have made me bawl.

I was at a party once, and went to the restroom to freshen up. When I came out, I continued smiling, mingling, having my picture taken. I was having a great time, but out of the corner of my eye, I could see my assistant waving at me like a madman. I waved back (who cares that we see each other ten hours a day—I'm happy to wave!). He shook his head and pointed to my butt. Uh-oh. I looked over my shoulder and realized that my dress was tucked into my G-string. Gulp. Who saw me? Did one of the tabloids get a picture of my naked ass? What kind of undies was I wearing? Oh god, do I have cellulite? I panicked, but then I realized that there was absolutely nothing I could do about the situation, so I just untucked my dress and burst out laughing and had a rocking time the rest of the night.

It's also sexy to laugh with other people. There's an idea out there that men like a woman who plays hard to get, who looks like the snottiest bitch in the room, but I've never found this to be true. Men are more attracted to women who will laugh at their jokes. When you're generous enough to listen to a man who is trying to impress you with his sense of humor and you laugh when something he says is funny, it makes him feel good— and besides, it's healthy for you to laugh anyway. Did you know that a study found that laughing raises energy expenditure and increases heart rate 10 to 20 percent? Translation: Ten to fifteen minutes of laughter could burn up to ten to forty calories per day, which could mean about four pounds a year. Plus, scientists say it reduces stress, improves circulation, stimulates the nervous system, heightens the immune system, and makes the heart stronger. So don't be such a cold fish. Loosen up and have a good time. People will be drawn to your sense of ease and they'll feel more comfortable around you if they see you as fun and human instead of as an ice queen.

Here's another thing that should make it easier. When you are actually into someone, his jokes are naturally funny to you . . . even if they're not. Dave cracked me up when we were first dating. Whatever he said I thought was interesting and funny. Five years later, he would tell the same old jokes to other people and I would groan, "Oh honey, not that joke again . . ."

Stand Tall

There's one very simple thing you can do to boost your inner confidence: Stand up straight and tall. It works every time. Have you ever felt good about yourself when you were slumped over? Didn't think so. You look better when you stand tall—thinner, more toned, and muscular—and you feel better because you're more aligned. My posture should be better than it is from all the ballet training I've had—I catch myself sometimes and I have to remind myself, *Pull up, shoulders back.* When I stand straight, I breathe deeper and slower and I can almost feel the tension drain from my neck and back and arms.

Turn Negative into Positive

When you're trying to muster up courage to calm your fears, use your anxiety to your advantage. Take all that energy and channel it into whatever you're doing. When you're fearful, you're also super alert and energized; yes, you're tense, but that tension can also be explosive. That's a lot of power you have at your disposal. The question is, are you going to let it drag you down or will you allow it to propel you forward? Here's a good example: You're on a first date and you're feeling nervous enough to pass out. You can a) run for the door while he goes to the little boy's room, b) put your head between your knees and try to stop hyperventilating, or c) hit the dance floor. You got it: Bust some moves. So what if you're shaking like a leaf? Maybe he'll think it's a new dance step. If you channel that nervous energy into physical energy, you'll not only work off some stress and steam, you'll probably wow him with your joie de vivre. Or at the very least, the music will be so loud, you won't have to worry about saying anything until you calm down . . . just dance, baby, dance!

Even a Flaw Can Be Fab

How boring would it be to go on a date with someone who was perfect? Imperfections are very attractive in people—I would never be attracted to someone who was a phony, a fake, who tried to hide what made him unique. Your true self is going to come out eventually anyway, so you might as well strip off all the pretenses from day one and let it all hang out. Let him fall in love with the person you truly are. Most people will relate to you more if you're human, and human is not perfect. People want to see your personality. It's not bad to be you. Embrace the little things that make you special, memorable. You're a klutz? I think that's cute. You're the world's worst cook? So what? That's what take-out is for. These are all little pieces—not the big picture. But they all help make you the person you are, and they're nothing to be ashamed of. Remember in *My Best Friend's Wedding* when the Cameron Diaz character can't carry a tune in karaoke but it only makes her fiancé love her all the more? Sure, we wanted Julia Roberts to get the guy . . . but you gotta admit, that off-key Cameron was cute as a button.

Look 'Em in the Eye

Even if you are frozen with panic and totally tongue-tied, a confident stare, straight in the eye, can camouflage it. I remember on my first date with Dave I giggled and smiled and didn't say all that much. But boy, did I look him straight in the eye with my best "come hither, you hottie" stare. That's my MO when I'm feeling insecure: I let my eyes do the talking. And boy, you wouldn't believe what a little eye contact can say: I'm interested, intrigued, impressed, in control, and totally into you.

Great Shakes

There is no greater turn off—in business or on a date—than someone who greets you with a bad handshake. What do I mean by bad? Some people shake your hand with a viselike grip (translation: "I am tough as nails; don't mess with me"). Others have a cold, clammy, wimpy grasp, like shaking hands with plate of linguini. Instant bad impression—and an instant giveaway that you're either insecure or overcompensating. So I asked the experts at New York City's Barbizon School (the people who coach modeling, poise, and all-around people skills) to break it down into a handshake how-to:

1. Keep your posture straight, make and maintain eye contact.
2. Step in toward the person when you shake hands; your grasp should be relaxed but firm.

3. Give a confident, sincere shake (about five seconds max), and, especially when in a stressful situation, make sure your palms aren't sweaty (a quick wipe on a cocktail napkin is a good precaution) before offering your hand.

4. To be ultra-demure you can turn your palm down and place only your fingers in his hand. Keep your chin down and your eyes up.

Now you have more than a few ideas of how to boost your self-esteem and feel good about yourself, your personality, your bod. Now it's time to radiate all those great, positive feelings outward, into a style befitting the newly fabulous you. The fun is just beginning . . .

take time to figure out what looks best on you. What works for me might not be right for someone else, so own it; be proud of what you like and what makes you feel good.

If you're feeling down, makeup has the ability to instantly lift your spirits. There's nothing like putting on a few coats of mascara and a drop-dead-red lipstick to make a girl feel better. I tend to accumulate tons of makeup—I guess I like to try new things, and I don't feel guilty picking up a $10 lipstick. So I have containers and makeup bags overflowing with products, but usually, I gravitate back to the tried-and-true faves: dark smoky rocker eyes, *big* bad-girl lashes, pale and glossy lips or red-hot red ones.

OVER THE YEARS I've picked up certain ways of doing my makeup from so many different artists. I may like how one person does my eyebrows or how someone gets my lips to look bigger and poutier. So I do a little of this, a little of that—my own makeup menu so to speak. And I believe that no matter how talented the artist is applying your mascara, you know your own face better than anyone else.

I know that makeup intimidates some women—maybe you're one of them. "Carmen," you moan, "I don't have a clue what to do with an eyelash curler. And whenever I put on a dark lipstick, I look like a hooker, not a hottie." Okay, honey, relax. I am so sure you can do this, I did it all myself, step-by-step, for you on these pages. You should have seen the reaction of the book people at the photo shoot: "What? She doesn't want a makeup or hair stylist? She's going to do it herself? Is she crazy?" But that's me—a DIY girl. And if you just take your time and experiment a little, not only will you create a sexy new look for yourself, you'll have a great time doing it. Makeup is playful; it's fun. Be daring, be willing to make mistakes (remember, it all washes off with a little soap and water). This will help you determine what

Makeup Musts

Karan Mitchell has been my makeup artist for many years. We have done commercials, calendars, magazines, award shows, you name it. She's amazing. She always makes my face look flawless—even if I have a breakout or didn't get much sleep—so you know I had to ask her to help me explain the best way to apply makeup and share some of her best celeb tricks and tips.

- Apply makeup in a well-lighted area.
- Remember the size of the brush you are going to be working with should correspond with the area of the face you are working with.
- A round brush is for blending. So it is always best to choose medium soft bristles of natural origin.
- Flat brushes are for applying color to a specific area with more intention, such as a line. You want a medium to hard bristle of synthetic quality. You don't want a natural bristle; this will absorb too much product.
- Make sure you pay close attention when selecting makeup brushes. Make sure the hairs are uniform and few loose ones are apparent.
- A good-quality brush can last up to five years. So take care of them as you would the hair on your head. A deep conditioning treatment once a month is a great idea.
- Always apply makeup to clean, moisturized skin.

looks best on you. Whatever style you choose, make it your own and enjoy what makes you feel good. And if you're still in need of a little inspiration, pick up a few magazines and thumb through them for ideas for daytime and nighttime looks.

Tips on Choosing Colors

It can be a little overwhelming to walk into a drugstore when you're looking for new cosmetics. Sometimes I feel paralyzed by the number of choices. It helps if you know going in what color palette looks most flattering on you, so you can narrow your search to the right range. And here's a quick tip to save you anguish and cash: If you are trying something new and bold, live in it for an hour. If it still doesn't feel right, it's not for you.

Eyeshadow

Matching eyeshadow to your eye color may seem like an easy choice, but it doesn't bring out your eyes ("make them pop") as much as a complementary color will. Here are some suggestions:

- BLUE EYES sparkle in shimmery metallic shades: gold, bronze, silver; also try mauve, brown-pink, and fleshy tones. My eyes are blue, and I love a terra-cotta shade.
- BROWN EYES look gorgeous in gold, bronze, khaki pewter, navy blue, mauve pink, and fleshy tones.
- GREEN EYES mesmerize in gold, bronze, gray, earthy tones, and fleshy tones.

Lipstick

I know some women who have twenty tubes of lipstick all in the same shade. If you love fuchsia and that's what makes you happy, then by all means wear it and be happy. Your lips are one area you can really experiment with (and I am a firm believer that any woman can wear red, any time, and feel completely sexylicious). But if you want a few guidelines from the pros, here goes:

- *If you have pale skin:* Stick to nudes, beige tones, light corals, and light pinks. Sheer formula lipsticks are also fabulous on fair skin—they look wet and tempting without overpowering.
- *If you have a medium skin tone/golden undertones:* All shades of red are for you. Also, brownish mauve, sheer burgundy, or spicy brown.
- *If you have dark skin:* Wear plums, chocolates, reds, and crimson-oranges. Generally, the deeper your skin tone, the deeper the shade of lipstick you can wear.

Blush

In order to keep those cheeks looking natural and not like Raggedy Ann, here's what makeup artists suggest:

- *For fair skin:* Look for beige, tawny, and pink tones.
- *For olive/yellow-toned skin:* Go for warm brown, almond, and copper shades.
- *For dark skin:* Opt for plum, auburn, and deep bronze shades.
- *For tanned skin:* Orange, apricot, peach, and coral shades look best.

Daytime Look

Every woman has a makeup routine, and, like the colors she chooses, it's intensely personal, but this particular look that I'm teaching you to apply here is a good starting point and should work for everyone. You can always intensify or tone down the look a bit if that's more your style. But I think it's a good face to put forward for work, the weekends, a casual date, etc.

Zapping Zits

I may be an actress, but I am not immune to the occasional vicious breakout. Pimples do not discriminate, and they have the knack for landing on your face at exactly the worst times. For me, it's usually right before a job interview, an audition, a photo shoot, an appearance on a talk show, or a big date. Remember, a pimple is an infected, clogged pore. The infection is what makes it red and painful. Skin has a cycle to repair itself, and it does, but sometimes we get a little anxious and try to help it along. If you cannot get to a great facialist for an emergency zap, there are a few things that will help. My solution is super easy and super cheap: I dip a Q-Tip in peroxide, touch it to the blemish, and usually by the next morning, that zit is history. It just really dries them up. Another plus—it's also good for cleaning ears. As for toothpaste on a zit, that's a BS urban legend. No actress piles Crest on her pimples. It doesn't work—trust me, I've tried. Karan swears by Listerine on a Q-Tip, which also works really well, without drying and burning. But if you have really torn one up on your face, because you couldn't leave it alone, you must treat the infection first, so that the skin can repair itself. Before going to bed, a dab of Neosporin on the bad breakout will help it along.

SKIN

Keeping Skin Healthy

It's like a cardinal sin to go to bed wearing your makeup; Karan would kill me if she knew that sometimes, I'm so exhausted, I pass out and forget to take off mine (hey, we all do it now and then). But any beauty expert will preach the importance of cleansing your face at night, and not just a quick splash of water—a really good wash to get off the dirt, grime, and goo.

Here's how to do it right:

1. First, find the right cleanser for your skin type. It doesn't have to cost a mint, it just has to do the job and make your face feel clean and look glowing. Most contain a mixture of oil, water, and other ingredients to break up the makeup and send it packing. You just have to find the right combo for you. And FYI, bar soaps tend to dry skin out, so avoid them, especially if you have dry skin to begin with.

2. You only have to cleanse before bedtime. A splash of warm water in the morning is sufficient. If you go overboard with your cleanser, you'll strip your face of the oils it needs and create dry, flaky skin.

3. Use warm—not hot or cold—water to rinse. Extreme temperatures can cause broken capillaries (those spidery red lines).

4. When you wash, splash your face with warm water first, then apply the cleanser (a dime-size dab will do ya) in a slow, circular motion, taking care not to rub too vigorously or get the cleanser into your eyes. Finish by removing the cleanser with a splash of cooler water to close the pores.

5. Exfoliate. Karan swears it's the key to a shine-free face. A gentle exfoliant daily helps to keep your pores and sebaceous glands, which secrete oil, working properly. You should try to avoid applying any makeup or moisturizer for at least an hour after exfoliating. The skin needs to be able to return back to its natural pH.

6. Moisturize. My name is Carmen Electra and I am a moisturizer addict. I cannot, will not, leave home without my moisturizer. I am neurotic about it. I use cocoa butter all over to keep my skin soft (there's nothing less sexy than rough elbows, scaly knees, or cracked heels). For my face, I use Enessa Aromatherapy's Facial Oil Balance Nourishments. I apply this oil every time I wash my face, and also first thing in the morning, before applying makeup, and again before bedtime. My skin just drinks it up. The right moisturizer can not only

reduce wrinkles and fine lines, but make your skin look and feel firmer, smoother, and more radiant. You have to find one that works for your skin type—dry, normal, oily, or combo— and use it religiously. I know a lot of girls who skip it, and it's a big mistake. Moisturizing sets your face up for the next steps and I really believe it prevents you from aging prematurely. Ever marvel at a sixty-year-old woman who looks like she's still in her forties? Betcha she's a member of Moisturizers Anonymous, too.

7. Stay well hydrated to nourish your skin and keep it supple. Replenish moisture inside and out. Drink plenty of water and eat healthy foods like vegetables (the brighter the colors of the veggies, the better they are for you). Green tea is another great beverage for your skin since it's packed full of antioxidants. I get my daily dose of green tea by taking NV Beauty Pill.

The Right Foundation

I use foundation every day—unless I'm going to the gym or hanging out around the house. Some women don't like foundation because they think it will feel heavy and masklike. It really depends on the kind you choose. Mine feels sheer and soft; it's a light, tinted base, and I don't even know it's on when I'm wearing it. It has just a hint of coverage, a hint of color. Which is all I need, since recently I've been having more girl time—BBQing and hanging out outside, getting some natural color from the sun. Of course you need to protect yourself with SPF to prevent cancer and wrinkles, but a touch of sun makes you feel good and it really makes your whole face come alive.

In general, I go a tiny bit warmer and deeper than my complexion because my body is tanner than my face and I like to match. But you may want to simply match your own natural shade. Not sure what this is? Karan showed me the best way to judge. Apply a swatch two or three shades of foundation along your jawline. One of the colors will simply disappear into your skin—that's your perfect match. Never test it on the back of your hand or the inside of your arm or anywhere else, because that's not the closest color to your face.

Many people like using their hands to apply foundation, some prefer a sponge, but I recommend applying it with this pink sponge shaped like an egg (it's actually called the Beauty Blender, but I just call it the egg). The egg is the bomb! Every woman should have an egg. It's good at blending and can really get into the eye area and under your nose.

I recommend a cream foundation for the T-zone across your forehead and down your nose and chin because that area needs more coverage. If you like your base more minimal, a great moisturizer and a powdered foundation applied with a big fluffy brush is great, too.

Cover Up

Next, I like to use a little cover-up under my eyes. For this one, I use my finger. That's how I learned to do it way back when at the Barbizon School of Beauty in Cincinnati when I was studying to be a model. I use my ring finger (second to last finger) because it's the

How to Be Sexy

weakest. Don't rub it in, just pat. You don't want to tug on the skin around eyes, because you don't want to stretch it. It's very thin, delicate skin. Tap, tap, tap is best.

Color is key here, too. My pet peeve is concealer that's too light. It makes you look older by giving you raccoon eyes. Mine is just a shade lighter than my base. I apply it in a small arc around the inside corner of my eye and then blend it down a little further along my cheekbones for a smooth effect (this is also a great way to cover up freckles if you don't like them). Again, blend it out by patting lightly, making sure not to pull or rub under the eye. Always blend concealer in the direction of the inner eye. I also put it in the frown area, just to soften up those fine lines.

Quick Tips

+ If you're using a brush for application be sure it is synthetic because synthetic brushes have a smoother texture and will not absorb the product.

+ Got a tiny flaw? Use a lighter shade as a primer on a scar, bruise, tattoo, or problem area. Then use the shade that matches your skin tone to blend in the area.

+ Pay special attention to any dark spots or circles on the inside corner of the eye and directly below the lash line.

Powder

I use two powders. First a lighter one that I put over any concealer, to seal it in place. Then, using a big, fluffy brush (I prefer a brush to a sponge because a sponge makes powder look a little too caked on and heavy), I go over my entire face and eyelids with the darker shade. I love a little hint of color in my

powder, too—I feel that it makes me look refreshed and alert even if I'm exhausted. It gives a nice, even look, an all-over glow. Again, you have to search out the shade that's perfect for you. Go too deep, and you'll look like a bottle of Orangina. Too light, and you can look pasty and pale. I suggest sweeping powder over your entire face and checking it in both natural and unnatural light (translation: check your bathroom mirror and take a peek in a compact outside in the sun). That's the only way to gauge if it's the right color. You can also ask a beauty consultant at a makeup counter for help, but I will be the first to admit I have gotten home more than once with a bag full of new makeup only to discover that when I put it on to go out that night, I looked jaundiced. You live, you learn . . .

EYES

Eyeliner

I'm definitely an eyeliner girl. I love how it shapes and defines my eyes. Eyeliner is meant to give depth to the lashes and make them appear thicker. The thickness and intensity of the eyeliner will depend on the size of your eyelid—the larger the eyelid area, the thicker and softer the eyeliner should be. As for lining below the eye, choose a shade that matches your eyebrow and stay close to the lash line.

I use black or dark brown to line the inside of my upper and lower lashes, all the way into both corners (or you can extend slightly outwards for an even more dramatic look) and then I use a small brush to blend and smudge, for a softer, smoky eye. You should feel free to go in with your fin-

gers, too. Pat McGrath, the brilliant makeup artist who did my Max Factor ads, used her fingers, and if Pat can, everyone else can, too. She's a genius.

Position the brush, pencil, or applicator as close to the lash line along the eyelid as possible. Begin the line from the center of the lid to the outside. Practice making it in one fluid stroke. Apply liner all the way around, then blend, baby, blend. At first, keep the line as thin as possible, and if you want a thicker line, repeat the process either across the entire lash line or simply on the outer third of the lid along the lashes. A great trick for a nice diffused line is to apply liquid liner first and then blend over it with a soft pencil or deep neutral eyeshadow.

There's no such thing as getting it wrong when you're doing a smoky eye. You can fix any line by smudging it.

Eye Shadow

My eye shadow color depends on two things: what I'm wearing and what mood I'm in. If I'm feeling a little edgy, bold, dramatic—I go for black and

charcoal gray. If I'm not feeling quite as intense, then I go with browns, and for a natural look, rose, salmony pink, or terra-cotta. Those shades really makes a light eye pop.

Practice your application and blend well; the goal is not to have obvious edges of color. Remember, lighter colors bring things forward and highlight, dark colors recede and add depth and shading. Try a few looks and take a few pictures. A little product in the right places can do wonders.

When applying an eye shadow, think first about the effect you want to achieve. Do you have deep-set eyes and want to make them appear larger? If so, you avoid hues that are deeper than your own skin tone.

Start by applying the shadow at the outside corner of the eye, not at the middle. This will make your color easier to blend. Shadows often comes as duos, trios, or quads, so if you have three different shades (dark, medium, and highlighter) use the medium one on the lid, the darkest in the crease and the highlighter on the brow bone. Again, blend them together to avoid a "rainbow" eye.

A good trick for blending your shadow is to begin at the base of the lash and work upward. And don't forget, you should use a clean brush for blending.

Mascara

I also think every woman looks more sexy and feminine with mascara. I love Max Factor Lash Perfection because it curls, separates, and really pumps them up. Since I have naturally long lower lashes, I only do the top during the day. For night, I add the bottom as well. Just make sure the mascara doesn't look too heavy or clumpy.

Always use a tissue to wipe excess mascara off the brush before applying to the lower lashes. Place your brush at the very base of your lash and wiggle it around, then brush through. You need a good coating of mascara at the base of the lash to keep them up. Use a lash comb or baby toothbrush to remove excess or clumps.

If you use a lash curler (and personally, I hate them and they scare the crap out of me), make sure it is completely free of old product and the rubber band is in its proper place (trust me, I have heard horror stories). The

greatest lash curler with be ineffective if any residue is left on the metal. It can also pull out a few of your lashes as well (yowch!). Squeeze at the base of the lash and count to five. Then make a second squeeze halfway up the lash, and apply mascara quickly after the curl.

Eyebrow

I used to fill in my eyebrows and tweeze them into perfect little arcs, but now I just let them grow. I think too much tweezing puts years on your face when you don't have a whole lot of eyebrow, so my feeling is more eyebrow is better than less. My mom plucked her eyebrows so much when she was young that they thinned completely and she always had to pencil them in; after a while, they didn't grow back. She still looked beautiful, but I'm hoping to keep my natural brows for life.

If you have thinner eyebrows, you might want to give them a boost and a little shaping. For shaping, choose a color that is slightly lighter then the color of your brows. First brush your brows into the shape you desire; fill in brows only where necessary. Don't draw over hairs that already exist. It's prettier to have a soft brow than a painted one. You should apply your brow powder, gel, or color using a stiff angle brush, working in the direction the hair grows.

How to Keep Lipstick from Kissing Off

Many makeup companies have created great lipsticks that stay on for hours (such as Max Factor's Everlites). But if you are the traditional lip pencil, lipstick, and gloss type, oil-blotting papers for the face are a great trick to use in between steps. First, apply a little balm. Blot. This leaves the essential emollients and removes excess oil or moisture. Line lips, blot, apply lipstick, blot, and tap a little gloss to the center to finish.

LIPS

Lip Pencil

A lip pencil is like an accessory—it's not totally necessary and everyone has her own preference. Some people apply lip liner after lipstick, and only where the natural lip line needs accentuating, but if you have trouble keeping your lipstick in place, line your entire mouth and fill it in as well.

I use a lip liner to make my lips look fuller, but try not to let it look too obvious. I'll go ever so slightly bigger than my actual lip line, but never too dark. If you feel you want the line to be diffused or even want to exaggerate your upper lip size, use your pinky and gently smooth out the liner.

Lip Color

A lipstick is as individual as the personality of the wearer. For day, I usually like a light pink lip. Many lip formulas today are so moisturizing you can almost skip the lip balm and the gloss. These are great to apply straight from the tube.

A Sexy Face

Apply lipstick in a thin coat with a lip brush and blot with a face blotting paper. Gently tap the areas you want to appear fuller—like the cushion of your bottom lip—with a touch of your concealer, and gently trace the new outline again with your lip liner. You can perfect the line with a Q-Tip dabbed in your foundation. To make it last even longer, try a lip stain as a base in the morning and then apply your shade on top.

Lip Gloss

I'm a gloss girl. There is nothing sexier than lips that look wet, soft, kissable. So no matter what shade of lipstick you choose, if you want to up the ooh-la-la quotient, just slick on a little gloss, put your lips together and pucker up . . .

How to apply gloss: Be it in a tube, a pot, a roll-on, or with a wand, you want to start with a dab of gloss in the center of your bottom lip. Don't think about putting it on all over like you do with your lip color; that will make your lips overly sticky or goopy. Just a dab will do ya. Then use a brush or wand to spread or simply press your lips together.

How to Be Sexy

CHEEKS

Blush

Blush adds color and life to your face. Ideally, you want it to look au naturel—flushed, like you've just had a fun session in the bedroom. You don't want red circles.

During the day, I don't like to overdo the blush, so I just add a touch of peachy shimmer on my cheekbones. Using a large, fluffy blush brush, apply the blush along the full line of the cheekbone and follow a smooth half moon stroke. Use a sponge to soften any hard edges. Apply the excess to the outside temple area, tip of the chin, side of the nose, or forehead, and sides of the neck.

If you're a newbie with brushes and powders use a tissue as your safety blanket. After you have loaded your brush with blush, rub the excess off on the tissue before you apply the color to your face.

Take It to Nighttime

It's a simple feat to take your day look to night—usually, all it requires is a little more color, intensity, and a more dramatic application. All I do is up the eyeshadow, intensify the blush, add false lashes, and pump up my lip color. And just go a little darker and thicker with the liner, extending up and out to make eyes look sexy and cat-like (very Brigitte Bardot). Like I said, easy.

False Eyelashes

For a night out, I love to play with false lashes (Ardell's Demi-Wispies or Fashion Lashes 112s are my faves and you can get them at the drugstore). With the right mascara, you don't need them, but they are a lot of fun, so I recommend you give them a try at least once.

A lot of women like the individual lashes, but strip lashes are so fabulous because with a little practice they are easy to apply. They are reusable and with all the styles available today, they can look natural or they can take your eyes from 0 to 60 in seconds! For a less dramatic look, you can cut them and use a smaller portion on the outer half of the lids. Always trim the strip lash to your eye size from the outside corner where the lash is longer.

The lashes with an invisible band are easiest to apply, so search those out when you're in the drugstore. To apply, squeeze lash glue evenly on the lash band—never on the lash itself. Wait a few seconds for the glue to become tacky. Position the lashes on as close to your lash line as you can without them poking you in the eye—you don't want to spend your night out on the town rubbing your eyes. Press the strip to the center of the eyelid first, then carefully place the outside down, followed by the inside. Tap into place.

These babies can get messy, so you want to practice ahead of time.

Eyeshadow

For a more intense color at night, go a little deeper with your eyeshadow. To get a deeper shade, wet your brush, and then mix it into the powder on your hand. Once the color is the shade you're looking for, swipe it across your lid and then blend away.

Lips

If you do a dramatic eye for night, it's usually better to keep your lips light. Otherwise, it's overload. But, sometimes, it's fun to be bold, bold, bold and go for a sassy red mouth. For intensive color that won't kiss off, draw a thin line along the edge of your lips with a lip liner in a shade slightly darker than

your lipstick. Start at the center of the upper lip and work outward. To make thin lips look fuller, line slightly outside the natural lip line. To make large lips look thinner, line slightly inside the lip line.

Next, apply lipstick straight from the tube or with a small, firm lip brush. Make sure to coat lips evenly and try not to smudge (if you do, concealer on a cotton swab will clean it up). Blot excess lip color with a tissue.

CHAPTER 4

Hair

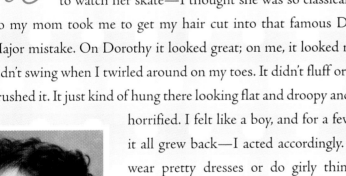

When I was about six, I was crazy about Dorothy Hamill. I loved to watch her skate—I thought she was so classically beautiful. So my mom took me to get my hair cut into that famous Dorothy bob. Major mistake. On Dorothy it looked great; on me, it looked ridiculous. It didn't swing when I twirled around on my toes. It didn't fluff or puff when I brushed it. It just kind of hung there looking flat and droopy and dead. I was

horrified. I felt like a boy, and for a few years—till it all grew back—I acted accordingly. I refused to wear pretty dresses or do girly things. It really messed with my head . . . literally and figuratively. So I swore from that day forth I would never, ever, chop my hair off again. Frankly, it's just not me. Which isn't to say cute little crops don't work wonders for Halle Berry or Sharon Stone. These ladies know how to carry it off and it looks gorgeous and powerful and sexy on them. But me,

I need big, long waves around my face and hair cascading down my back to make me feel va-va-va-voom. And even though, at some point, my hair has probably been every color of the rainbow, I think some version of light brown is me.

No one knows your hair like you do. Don't ever let any overzealous hairstylist convince you that he knows best what style works on you. He can make suggestions—suggestions are good—but you are the one who has to walk out of that salon feeling like a million bucks. I have had a lot of stylists try to "arrange" my hair into some intricate 'do with dozens of hairpins and gallons of spray, mousse, or gel. "Hairdos" are so old-fashioned. They make you look older, no matter what age you are. Youthful hair is soft and natural. I hate helmet hair. I hate hair that is so untouchable—not to mention flammable—that you feel as if it's weighing you down all night. I prefer a natural look. It's more youthful and vibrant. I think sexy hair is slightly undone or unkempt; think Brigitte Bardot bedhead. Think of the way your hair looks—wild and wicked—after you've just had a passionate roll in the hay. I love my hair to evoke that feeling. Whether I wear my hair pulled back, piled up, or in a pony, there are always a few strands just doing their own thing.

It's so cool that nowadays you can change your hairstyles as easily as you do your undies. There is haircolor that washes in—and out—in a few shampoos. There are amazing hair extensions that look so real, you can have hair down to your butt today and a close-crop mañana. There are amazing tools that can straighten, curl, or crimp in a few minutes. And there are products that can gloss, texturize, and revitalize.

One of my favorite hairstylists, Jim Crawford, explained to me that in the end, the hairstyle that's right for you is not just one that looks good, but one that works with your life. If you're a frazzled working mom, chances are you're going to go for a style that is easy to just wash and wear—not some complicated look that requires a lot of primping. And if you're a high-powered biz exec, you're probably looking for something that's conservative, sleek, and sophisticated. Versatility is also key—you don't want a haircut that looks the same every day (yawn). You want something that you can style a few different ways—depending on what mood or style strikes you.

I Think I'm Ready for a Radical New 'Do

Good for you. Here are some of Jim's best tips for biting the bullet:

1. Summer is the best time to make a huge hair change. That's because the summer months are your fastest growing season (hair will grow a half inch to an inch a month during warm weather versus only a quarter to a half inch a month in the fall-winter season). So in case your stylist screws up and you hate it, it will grow back twice as fast.

2. Before you decide on your 'do, do your homework. Check out pictures from fashion magazines to show your stylist. You can use one whole look or the bangs from one, the length from another, and the sides from yet another picture. Or watch women on the street. Do you like someone's look? Don't be shy; ask where she got her cut and if she liked the hairdresser and the salon.

3. Make a list of what you are looking for in a hairstyle. Is it versatility? Easy styling? A shape that makes your face look slimmer or younger? A cut that is more polished and professional? Write down a list of adjectives to describe your ideal look: cute, coy, sexy, simple, soft, show-stopping.

4. Make an appointment for a hair consultation, either a half-hour before the actual cut or on a separate day. Try not to be intimidated;

remember your hairdresser is there for you (you're paying him or her to make you look great). You are in control, and you shouldn't feel pressured to do something you don't want to do (like chop off six inches or dye your hair red). A good hairstylist is always willing to "collaborate" with you on your look. Yes, the stylist's an expert, but shouldn't be a bully. If you feel as if he or she doesn't listen to you, then take your hair—and your money—elsewhere.

Rx for Perfect Hair

Every hairstylist seems to come equipped to every shoot with a doctor's bag filled with potions and products for curing what ails your hair. Jim recommends the following:

- a lightweight spray lotion or mousse to give your hair added shine and protection
- a great lightweight hairspray or finishing spray to control any fly-aways and to give support in bad weather
- a paddle brush for smoothing strands straight when blow drying
- a medium and large round brush for shaping layers or angling hair while drying
- a wide-tooth comb (for unsnarling tangles)
- hairpins, bobby pins, and elastic bands to hold every hair in place

FIVE GREAT TIPS FOR GREAT HAIR

1. Use a shampoo and conditioner that is right for you hair type and texture. Your hair will thank you. It doesn't have to be super pricey

Shape Smarts: The Best Cuts for Your Face Shape

The shape of your face is the best guide for what type of cut will work for you. Look at your face in the mirror and use an eye pencil to trace the shape.

OBLONG

What works: Short or medium lengths; soft wispy bangs (makes your face look fuller); layering on the sides (again, creating fullness)

What doesn't work: Long hair (it "pulls" the face down); closely cropped hair

OVAL

What works: Lucky you—you have the perfect-shaped face. Almost any style will look great on you. A few to consider: sleeker styles for evening (partial updos, chignons, or slicked-back layers) to show off your face shape

What doesn't work: Bangs that are too heavy or shaggier styles that hang in your face—this makes it lose its shape

ROUND

What works: Fuller styles that have height at the crown. Cute flips, wispy bangs, fringy cuts that angle in toward the face, minimizing the "moon" shape

What doesn't work: Chin-length hair that is rounded like your face (a bob); it will only make your face look wider

HEART-SHAPED

What works: You are blessed with fabulous cheekbones, girlfriend. Work 'em. A classic chin-length bob—especially a swingy one—looks great; side-parted styles also work well (they minimize the fullness of your forehead); side-swept bangs

What doesn't work: Too-short styles. They will make your chin look too pointy.

SQUARE

What works: Any style that softens the angles of your face. Soft waves, wispy layers, and bangs. Short to medium lengths look best.

What doesn't work: Too-straight styles or anything too sleek or severe.

either. Just read the label carefully; consider your hair type (oily, dry, combo); texture (fine, frizzy, thick); and condition (healthy, color-treated, fried). But don't get married to one shampoo or conditioner for too long either. Experts say you should switch it up now and then, to wake your hair up and readjust its pH levels.

2. Same goes for products: gels, lotions, and hairsprays should be chosen according to your hair's needs, not just what's on sale this week at the drugstore. Yes, it takes a little extra effort to sort through all those bottles and sprays, but in the end, if your hair looks less poodlelike and more professional, isn't it worth it? As a general rule of thumb, mousses add lightweight volume and control to layered looks; gels control curls or create slick and sleek wet-looking styles; pomades are for textured, funky, and spiked styles. Finally, a hairspray seals the deal: Go for a light hold if you like hair to move and swing; an extra-strong hold if you want it to keep its shape, even in a tornado.

3. Not all hairbrushes are created equal. Brushing both cleans and massages the scalp and stimulates the release of sebum (an oil at the base of the hair follicle) that moisturizes and makes hair healthier. Brushing also cleans the hair and scalp by removing dirt. That said, you need to use the right brush for your hair type and length. The idea is to use a brush that gives you the finished look you desire—be it straight, wavy, or somewhere in between. Personally, I love my Mason Pearson brush. It really shapes and styles my hair without pulling it out.

    A hair brush made with boar or nylon bristles—although probably a little more expensive—is better for your hair and will probably last longer. Brushes that are made with cheap plastic bristles tend to be stiffer and can scratch the scalp if the ends of the bristles are badly made and pointed, instead of round. You should clean your brush regularly (remove the hairs, then rinse with warm water and a mild soap or shampoo); replace your brush once a year.

Hairbrushes 101

+ ROUND BRUSHES give you a lift (volume) and a slight bend to the hair. The barrels of some round brushes are ceramic based to help cut your drying time in half by retaining more heat from your blow-dryer.

+ PADDLE BRUSHES or any flat brush with a lot of bristles keeps your hair straight with maximum tension.

+ VENT BRUSHES dry your hair quicker since there are vents cut in behind the bristles. They give you a more natural look because of the minimum amount of tension.

+ PLASTIC BRISTLE brushes allow your hair to slide through the bristles without any pulling or snagging. Be sure to find one with rounded bristle ends.

+ BOAR BRISTLE brushes are gentle on the hair and scalp (and help to distribute natural oils) and have natural antistatic properties to help eliminate static electricity in the hair.

+ TOURMALINE-INFUSED brushes help repair the hair follicles. This reduces brittleness and helps to keep hair static-free.

+ ION-INFUSED brushes and combs fight frizz and make your hair smooth and shiny.

4. The right hot tools. There are some great curling and straightening irons out there—and you don't have to spend hundreds of dollars anymore to own one (many of the new ceramic models are under $40). Jim loves the ones that have a temperature control so that you can heat it up in split seconds. You can then "dial the style" based on your hairtype (fine, medium, tough to curl, etc.). Some can be used on slightly damp hair to save time when you're rushing to be somewhere.

5. No matter what condition your hair is in, trim it every six to eight weeks. No excuses. Not only will it keep your style's shape, but it will remove fried ends, which can further split up the shaft.

Hair How-tos

DAY LOOKS

These are really my favorite hairstyles for two reasons. First, they always look glam without being too "done." And second, they are a cinch to do. I promise.

Big, beautiful hair with "natural" waves

Products: Bumble and Bumble Surf Spray and hairspray
Tools: Blow-dryer, curling iron, and a medium round brush

This is a good choice for everyday wear and for any hair type or texture. After washing, use conditioner. Put in Surf Spray with hair still wet; it

gives it more texture, so the hair feels thicker (like you've just gotten out of the ocean) and you can style it more easily. Blow-dry using your hands only, flipping your head upside down and from side to side to help create texture and volume at the root of the crown. You need to start with a voluminous, full head of hair because the volume always decreases as the day goes on. And if you have poker-straight hair like me, without proper prep, the curl tends to fall out the second you step out the door.

Part your hair down the middle, then gather most of your hair on the top of your head and tie it in a knot (which is great because you don't have to mess with pins) leaving just the bottom layer. If your hair won't hold a knot, grab a hair tie and some pins and pull it back.

Then curl your hair section by section. Take about a one- to two-inch section and brush through it. Clamp the hair about two inches above the ends and curl it straight up and down. Leaving the ends free will give you a more natural look. I use a special curling iron called Hot Tools (you can get

one at a beauty supply store), which curls quickly. Don't hold it too long or you'll burn your hair.

Hold it straight up, pull straight down. This gives you a natural looking curl, not a tight finger curl.

Once the hair is cool, grasp the same section of hair again at the root, then roll it close to your head straight up and down, then pull it straight down and out again. This is something I made up that works for me. Maybe it will work for you, too.

Make sure the hair is cool before you go back in. Make your way gradually around your head, and then let down the next layer of hair.

Working from the bottom up, repeat until you've curled all the hair. If there are long pieces, go back in and curl close to the ends to keep it from looking ratty.

How to Be Sexy

Next, pull all your hair up on the back of the crown and secure with a silicone- or cloth-covered rubber band.

Using a small bit of pomade, smooth flyaways on the top and sides of your hair, but don't use it on the ponytail (or it will droop quickly).

Take a one-inch section of hair from the ponytail and back comb or tease it using your finger. Spray the length of hair with hairspray and wrap around the base of the ponytail to cover the rubber band and to give a more polished look. Then secure the ends after you have wrapped the section of hair around the base of the pony with hairpins.

Now for the pony: Alternate between a medium- and large-barrel curling iron using one-and-a-half inch sections of hair. Apply hairspray

to each section before you curl it, then wrap the hair from the roots to the ends, leaving just the tips of the hair out of the curling iron.

For an extra high ponytail, use one of those fabulous little clips. Break the pony in half, and then use the clip to clasp the top half of the hair. Release the clip and then pull the hair over it to hide it, creating a cute, perky bump.

When you are done, run your fingers through the ponytail to soften and blend the waves. This is a great and easy look for anyone on the go.

EVENING LOOK

Red-hot retro
   Products: spray-on gel and hairspray
   Tools: blow-dryer, paddle brush, large-barrel curling iron

This is a look for any evening adventure. Start by applying the spray gel all over the head from the roots to the ends of your hair. Using a generous amount (but not too much) of product will help to make the look more polished with less flyaway's and give your curl more lasting power.

Using a large flat paddle brush blow-dry your hair from the center part to the ends, keeping your hair as smooth and flat as possible. Dry in this direction till completely dry. When the hair is completely dry, take one-inch sections of hair starting at the nape of the neck and spiral the section around the curling iron from the roots to the ends of the hair leaving one inch of the ends uncurled. Do this on the whole head until you reach just above the ear area; from there up take your sections and start two inches from the root area and wrap the hair around the curling iron. This will give you wave and curl throughout the strand of hair without giving you curl at the roots, which is where you don't want it. When you're done with the whole head rake your fingers or a very wide-tooth comb though your hair to blend the sections of curled hair together. Spray lightly to control any flyaways.

CHAPTER 5

Style

Audrey Hepburn had her little black dress. The Fonz had his leather jacket. And Jessica Simpson has made those Daisy Dukes and cowboy boots work wonders for her. Then there are people like Gwen Stefani who take chances and are never afraid to mix bold patterns or colors or like Kate Moss who, with undone hair and natural makeup, always look effortlessly great.

Signature style is about personal expression. Your clothes and accessories should reflect the person you are (or want to be) and getting dressed should be fun, a pleasure, not a chore, every day.

Okay—I am not unfamiliar with this scenario: You look in your closet and see nothing—positively nada—to wear. Nothing fits, matches, isn't covered with stains or wrinkled beyond belief. There were many years when I had zero disposable income to blow when that feeling hit me, so how did I manage to develop any sense of style—much less a signature look to call my own?

I won't lie to you—I shopped. I shopped a lot. And I still love to shop.

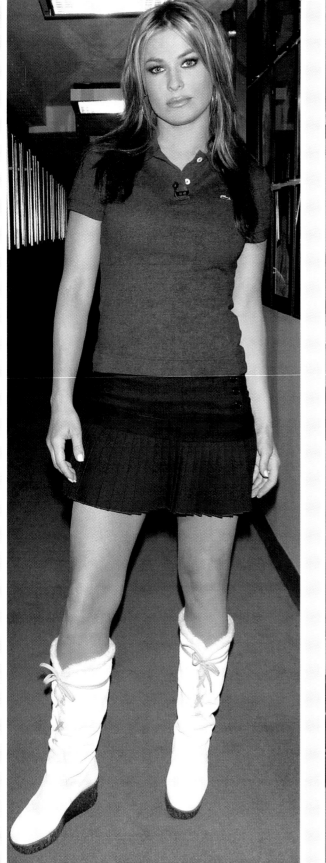

I've just become a lot smarter about it. I am not grabbing stuff off racks or scooping up labels. I actually know what looks good on me. Style is a direct reflection of how you feel about yourself—it's the image you want to put forth to the world, so it truly reflects what's going on inside your heart and head.

Some people have called me a style chameleon and I like that—it's fun to change your look from year to year, or even day to day, and unpredictable is always sexy. I guess you could say that "sexy/ unpredictable" is my signature style.

I'm lucky, because I go to events and parties and award shows and people are nice enough to lend me fabulous clothes. Sometimes, I feel as if I'm playing dress up, just like I did when I was a little girl, but this time, the diamonds are real and the gowns are couture. It doesn't get much better than that, and I'm grateful for it every time I look in the mirror before a night out on the town.

Photo shoots are really fun. I actually like having my picture taken—artsy, edgy, fashion-forward shoots are my favorites. Even though I'm usually a shy person, somehow when I'm posing in a bikini that leaves little to the imagination, I can turn on my inner sex goddess and act the

I WANT CANDY 2007

part. But as much fun as the modeling is, I'm always nervous to see the final pics. Sometimes I think they look amazing; other times, I look at them and I'm like, "Oh, god. That sucks!" I guess I'm a little bit of a perfectionist when it comes to myself.

It's easy to look at what other people are wearing—check out a celebrity in a magazine or note what your friends are sporting around the office—and just copy it. But that's not style; that's cookie-cutter. There's no originality, and no personality, to following what someone else is doing (and frankly, tube tops, gauchos, and platforms just don't

How to Be Sexy

Mischka gown. Strapless—very feminine for me at the time.

So now sometimes I go soft and refined, other times I go wild and edgy. Those are two sides of my personality that I let loose in my outward appearance. It's important to assess what side of yourself you want to project before you even think of overhauling your style. Are you secretly a daring dominatrix who wants to dress in head-to-toe leather? Or are you the princess type, who prefers a pretty, flowy dress and ladylike pearls (with lots of lace underneath it all)? Or are you both? That's fine, too. I happen to think leather and lace work really well together. And listen to what your body is telling you. There are certain days of the month when I am not feeling my skinniest, and there is no way I am going out of the house poured into a short, tight dress.

And it works the other way around, too. Sometimes when you put on a certain hot outfit, it instantly lifts your mood. During the shoot for this book, I was feeling blah on the first day. I had just gotten back from a trip to Turkey, I was a little sick, and just generally having a hard time. Shooting photos was the last thing I wanted to do—which is really not like me. I went through my normal makeup routine, but I just wasn't into it. But when it was time to

How to Be Sexy

switch up my look, I painted on a red mouth, changed my clothes, and suddenly, it was like an electric charge went through me. I shook off my funk and got into what I was doing. Everyone noticed. The photographer said I'd finally come to life and I started loving it. It was a great example of how an exterior change can jump-start an interior one.

Your Personal Style File

It would be fabulous if some fashion fairy godmother could appear one day with a killer Dolce Gabanna gown and Louboutin heels and, *poof!*, turn you into an instant style queen. Like everything in life, you have to learn through experience, and in this case experimentation.

If you follow these tips you will eventually hone a style sixth sense. You'll instinctively know what works on you and doesn't. You'll find go-to pieces that you can always pull out of your closet when you need to feel sexy.

TIP 1: WINDOW SHOP TILL YOU DROP

Ladies, you should take advantage of the beauty of the try-on. You can check out dozens of styles and looks to figure out what is most flattering—for free! Lots of women bring along a camera when they're shopping for wedding dresses, and there's no reason why you shouldn't use this trick when you're shopping for a signature style. Digital cameras have made this a no-hassle experience. You can load the images into your computer and figure out a wardrobe just like Cher in *Clueless*.

And if you're completely clueless about fashion, I promise you can learn. I did. I used to spend hours poring over style.com looking at the runway collections to get new ideas or see what the hot trends were. I still do.

The Best Pieces for Every Shape and Size

Face it—no woman is 100 percent happy with every inch of her bod. I'm not. You're not. Even Heidi Klum probably hates something about herself (although I can't imagine what). Hooray for fashion—the instant figure fixer. Just choosing certain styles can magically camouflage any little flaws (or even big ones).

FOR WIDE HIPS (AKA A PEAR SHAPE)

Choose: A-line skirts (they fit loosely around the hips and draw the eye away from the problem); jackets that fall to mid-thigh length; sleeveless or strapless necklines that draw the eye upward and put the focus on your upper—rather than your lower—half; fuller, wide-leg pants. The goal is to find clothes that gently skim the hips and butt and take the emphasis off your bottom half.

Avoid: miniskirts; cargo pants (pockets at hips or on the butt call attention to those areas); cropped tops or jackets that end at the waist; ruching or cinched-in belts (this makes the hips look fuller).

FOR BIG BREASTS

Choose: V-neck tops, boatnecks, open-collar tops; an A-line skirt to balance out your top; short skirts (to draw attention to great legs and away from your top half); slender pants (no pleats). The idea is to balance out your top-heavy figure and draw the eye down.

Avoid: too tight or too big tops; puffy or dolman sleeves (make you look more top-heavy); strapless or spaghetti strap dresses (unless you have a great bra or the top is a corset-style with adequate built-in support).

FOR A TUMMY BULGE

Choose: ruched dresses (they pull you in at the middle and the pleats camouflage a multitude of sins); V-necks that draw the eye upward; ruffled tops that hide the stomach behind layers of loose fabric; tapered jackets; narrow or boot-cut pants; tunic-style tops and sweaters.

Avoid: narrow belts, drawstrings, cropped-tops; pleated pants; tight-fitting shirts.

TIP 2: SEXY DOES NOT MEAN SLUTTY

Most stylists have always advised me that less is more. If you go for a plunging neckline that showcases your double-Ds, keep your bottom half covered up. If you want to wear a micromini skirt that spotlights shapely legs, then wear a conservative neckline. And you never, ever want to wear something so risqué that you risk pulling a Janet Jackson at the company Christmas party. Yes, if you got it, flaunt it, but do so tastefully (that double-sided tape can do wonders to keep everything where it belongs; one side sticks to the skin, the other to the fabric).

TIP 3: ASK FOR OPINIONS

I have my own thoughts on what I like to wear and what looks good on me, but I've also worked with some amazing designers and stylists who have helped me shape my style over the years. Sometimes I completely disagree with them and I assert the right to veto (hey, it's my bod, not yours, in that dress). But other times, they inspire me to try something new, something I would never see as "me," and not only do I like it, I love it. It's good to have an objective opinion now and then—from a spouse, a friend, a sister, a mom. Anyone will do as long as they know you well and aren't color-blind.

TIP 4: FEEL THE FASHION

Here's some great advice a stylist once gave me: Put on the clothes and think about how they make you feel. Feminine and beautiful? Or like a bad-ass? Can you move in the clothes comfortably, or is the cut too tight and constrictive, so you feel awkward or fat? How 'bout the color: Does that hue make you look radiant—or sick? Do you like what you see? Do you feel tall, confident, cool, and chic? Honey, it's a keeper. And that's what you want to fill your wardrobe with, clothes that make you feel great about yourself, which show off all your best features and cleverly hide what ever bags, sags, or sticks out when and where it shouldn't.

TIP 5: YOU DON'T NEED TO SPEND A FORTUNE

Great clothes do not necessarily need to have a hefty price tag attached to them. A hot label doesn't guarantee you a great fit. Buy yourself a designer ensemble or accessory if it makes you feel good, but don't feel that you need a name on your bod in order to have sexy style. I know some amazingly sexy women who frequent flea markets, vintage boutiques, and discount department stores. And guess what? They always look like a million bucks when they've probably spent under $100. The secret to looking like you spent $500 when you've really spent $50? Tailoring. A good tailor will be able to make the clothes skim your body as if they were custom-made. Sure, this will cost you an additional $20 or so per item, but it will be well worth the investment to have clothes that look as if they were literally made for you.

TIP 6: WHAT YOU WEAR *UNDER* THERE COUNTS

Now, I ask you, how could you ever feel sexy wearing a ratty ol' pair of white cotton briefs? Even if no one can see what you've got under that low-cut little black dress or your track suit, *you* know. And if those nasty knickers don't squash your mojo, I don't know what will. Toss them—there is never an occasion for unsexy undies. Go out and stock up on the prettiest pairs (five should do you for starters) and matching bras or camis—lace ones, satin

ones, polka dot, leopard spot, embroidered, sequined, embellished. You can be dainty or daring. And don't forget garter belts, merry widows, corsets, even crotchless. I just love lingerie and can't get enough of it. It gives me an instant psychological boost knowing that I am wearing sexy little panties. One of my girlfriends says you should always wear underwear that wouldn't embarrass you if you end up hooking up with a guy spur-of-the-moment. Remember when Renee Zellweger as Bridget Jones is rolling around on the floor with Hugh Grant and he reaches under her skirt to find her hideous suck-it-all-in girdle? Perish the thought.

TIP 7: HEAD TO TOE, YOU SHOULD GLOW

In other words, never neglect your hygiene and grooming. Make sure your hair isn't stringy or greasy—unless you're going for that grunge look; your nails aren't chipped or bitten to the quick; your feet aren't rough and callused (the Band-Aids on the heels are usually a dead giveaway). First of all, pampering and primping will make you feel good. Second of all, it's one of the first things a guy will notice about you—way before he sees that trendy little dress. But there is an exception to this rule: Sometimes I like to wear jet-black chipped nail polish—very rocker cool. I'm comfortable with that style. But unless you can pull off this vibe with bravado, a weekly mani/pedi and monthly hair trim can work wonders for your appearance and your ego. And don't underestimate how great a really dark color—like Vamp or Plum or Wicked—or a black and white French manicure can look with even a buisiness suit. You gotta try it before you pass judgment.

TIP 8: FIND ONE FAB ITEM AND BUILD AROUND IT

Unsure where to start on your quest for a style persona? All you need is one piece of clothing per outfit—a basic black dress, some hot designer jeans, a

A change of accessories takes this dress from day to night.

How to Be Sexy

flattering A-line skirt—to serve as your foundation. Whatever you choose should make you feel your sexiest (and if you love it all that much, I strongly suggest buying one or two more in another color). Now add on the rest of the outfit and the accessories, always using your fab item as the center of your style universe. When you have a little more money to splurge, add a few more fab pieces—but there's no need to go crazy and buy everything new all at once. It's easy to go from day to night if you have the basics and you love to accessorize.

10 Sexy Pieces Every Woman Needs in Her Wardrobe

Amanda created this little checklist for me—she says that if you have these basics in your closet, you'll always be stylish.

1. A pair of black, closed-toe, two- to three-inch heels. They go with anything—even jeans. And the heel height won't leave you crippled if you're on your feet all day. Look for leather, which will stretch and breathe the most and be the most comfortable, as opposed to other materials such as vinyl.
2. A pair of slimming, dark denim jeans. The cut and the waist don't matter. As long as the wash is a deep midnight blue and they fit you like a glove.
3. A V-neck cashmere sweater. A little loose, and a little plunging. What man wouldn't like to put his arms around a girl wearing this? Choose a color that flatters your complexion—vibrant red or ultraslimming navy or black are usually best.

4. A pair of diamond stud earrings (real or faux). Every girl feels like a princess in these, and they add instant glamour, even to a T-shirt and sweats.

5. A great bra that really fits. Go and get measured; try one on and look at yourself from all angles, and make sure it does what it's supposed to do: lift, separate, support, and minimize or maximize.

6. Sexy panties. Lacy, leopard print, G-string. You name it. They can even be cheap, as long as they make you feel naughty under even the most conservative attire. They're an instant confidence booster, not to mention your very own dirty little secret.

7. An A-line skirt. Universally figure-flattering. If you are voluptuous, keep the length longer. If you have great legs, go for a mini. The color and fabric don't matter either—as long as you love it.

8. A little black dress. The style—strapless, cap-sleeved, long-sleeve, is completely up to you. But simple and elegant is key; no froufrou touches or flashy details. You can always dress it up with accessories.

9. A great everyday bag. One that is made well, in a good material with nice hardware. It should be big enough to carry all your essentials yet shouldn't be so big people mistake it for luggage. Again, price is not important here: you don't have to break the bank on the latest Marc Jacobs. Just look for a style that suits you—be it a satchel, sling, or backpack.

10. A great evening bag. A simple black satin clutch or a gold or silver beaded one goes with everything—and adds instant glamour to even the most mundane black suit or dress.

CHAPTER 6

Body Language

I am a lip licker. And a hair tosser. And sometimes I bat my eyes. These are the ways I show someone that I am a) interested, b) having fun, or c) feeling naughty. Sometimes I do these movements unconsciously; other times, I deliberately use a gesture to communicate something that maybe I'm just too shy to blurt out at that moment. A guy might pick up a signal from me without my saying a word. That's due to the amazing science of kinesics. Translation: the study of body language. Of course, this science is not completely infallible: sometimes, a gesture can mean more than one thing. For example, just because I cross my arms doesn't necessarily mean I wish you'd crawl under a rock. Maybe it's just cold in the room. And of course, you can misread a gesture entirely. Once, this guy I had a crush on leaned back in his chair and I thought, "Okay, I've lost him." Instead, he just had a backache from working out and was trying to stretch out the kinks. Luckily for me, he flared his nostrils a few seconds later—a sure sign that he was into me.

The study of body language has been around for a while: Charles Darwin first wrote about it in his book *The Expression of the Emotions in Man and Animals* published in 1872. And ever since, there have been lots of studies about it, and researchers have found enough evidence for me—and hopefully you—to take it seriously. A recent BBC series on the subject reported that it takes us between ninety seconds and four minutes to decide if we like someone. Wow. That means the length of your average commercial break is about all you got to show your true self. Fifty-five percent of the impression we get from someone comes through our body language; 38 percent is from the tone, speed, and inflection of our voice; and a mere 7 percent is from what we're actually saying. So who needs witty repartee, right? Send out the right signals and you'll have your man hooked before you even open your mouth. And if you're having any doubts that he's not feeling amorous, you can read his body language to see where his head is at.

The Seven Signs That Say "I'm Hot for You"

I asked a body language expert, Robert Phipps (www.bodylanguagetraining.com), to help me highlight a few of the basics. But there have been a ton of books written on the topic—so if you're so inclined, you can do even more homework and become an expert yourself.

1. THE EYEBROW RAISE. When you catch someone's gaze from across the room, smile and raise both eyebrows in a quick flash then lower them (Mr. Big on *Sex and the City* perfected this move). This is a sign, say the experts, of interest, excitement, and arousal. Just make sure to

raise both brows simultaneously; a solo brow raise is a sign of anger, skepticism, or doubt.

2. THE COPY CAT. When you like someone, mimic his moves. If he leans forward, you lean forward. If he strokes his chin, you stroke yours. The idea is to mirror him in a way that conveys intimacy and synchronicity. Just make sure you're only copying his positive gestures—and don't be too obvious about it. Wait a few beats before you mirror and do it subtly, or it may look like mocking, not mimicking.

3. THE BLINK. If you like something you're looking at it, your eye blinks more frequently. So when you're talking to that super stud at the bar, try blinking more (just don't get carried away or he'll think you've lost a contact lens). If he blinks more himself in response, *bingo!* The boy is attracted.

4. THE LIP LICK. When it doubt, wet your whistle. This is a direct sign of sexual interest. As is a lip pucker (looks like your ready for a kiss). Just don't bite your lips—this, according to the experts, means you're nervous, afraid to speak, or hoping he'll shut up soon.

5. THE FULL-FRONTAL LEAN. Think of this as a little flirty hokey-pokey maneuver. Ya put your whole self in . . . this indicates you're both eager to hear what he has to say and also eager to get close, closer, closest with every inch of your being. Sitting in a chair? Ever so slowly slide forward, and move your head, shoulders, knees, toes . . . you name it, toward him. By far, the clearest of body language moves. If he doesn't get this one, the only thing left to do is jump in his lap.

6. THE HAIR TWIRL. As you're giving that guy across the room "a look," slowly wind a few strands of hair seductively around your fingers. Got his attention? Now run your fingertips through your hair, like a sex kitten preening her fur. A hair toss also works well: simply toss one side over your shoulder, then the other (Cher made this an art form). Just remember to keep your moves slow, seductive, and

tied). At the very least, it indicates insecurity, fear, or close-mindedness.

4. THE PULL AWAY. Does your conversation resemble a seesaw? He leans forward, you lean back, and vice versa? You two are probably not a match made in heaven. If you're putting miles between you, it's probably a sign that you're wishing he'd walk.

5. THE STATUE. Yes, standing tall is a sign of confidence. But someone whose posture is rigidly straight for several minutes (think Buckingham Palace guards) is trying to tell you "buh-bye." This is even more effective with hands crossed across the chest or resting firmly on the hips. A stiff bod is also a dead giveaway that you're nervous; when you're ill at ease, you look uncomfortable (and probably are).

6. THE MOUTH COVER-UP. Okay, maybe you were just stifling a yawn or silencing a belch. These things happen. But usually, placing your hand over your mouth is a sign that you are not telling the truth. "Oh, sure, we could go out some time . . ." you say before placing a palm to your lips. Take a hint, Romeo: It will never happen.

7. THE NOSE NUDGE. It wasn't an itch that sent his fingertips to the side of his nose. Experts say if it's done when someone is speaking to you, it indicates they're lying. Another nose negativity: the wrinkle. Cute as it may be in a *Bewitched* kinda way, it means you're grossed out by the guy or something he just said or did.

Strike a Pose

Models and Madonna aren't the only ones who can Vogue. Every woman can and should learn several basic seductive positions/postures to use when walking, standing, or sitting. Not only are you guaranteed to look great in

An A-List Pose

Ever notice that some celebrities always seem to pose in the same way? Maybe chin down and angled left . . .? That's because they know what head position looks best for them. Try these on for size:

+ Look to the left, then to the right. Now smile. Which side of your face do you feel looks more like "you"? That's your best side.

+ Now, tilt your chin down—then, with chin down, look to the left and right again.

+ Finally, try a diagonal tilt left and right.

+ Make sure your eyes convey what you want expressed.

+ Practice in front of a full-length mirror so you can see the full view of what everyone else sees.

pictures, but should Mr. McDreamy glance your way at the office Christmas party, he'll be mesmerized. For this one, I asked the place that first taught me to model when I was eleven years old, way back in 1983, the Barbizon School of Modeling, for a quick refresher course. My Cincinnati school's owner, Sharon Camposeo, and also the NYC branch, owned by Jay and Cathrine Goldstein, were happy to oblige. Some of these moves I kinda just do naturally now—like the over-the-shoulder glance. Others, I'm happy they pointed out to me—so I know better next time how to sit when giving an interview. (Shocker! Not cross-legged.)

And here's my own personal advice on how to inspire yourself: Honey, if you wanna work the catwalk like a real diva, rent yourself the video *Paris Is Burning*. Those bitches really know how to work it!

How to Be Sexy

You can also achieve the same pose on the opposite side simply by changing the right and left foot as front/back foot etc.

THE RUNWAY WALK

Sure, we've pretty much all walked from the age of one, but are we all doing it to look sexy? Do you look like your best, most confident self?

1. Start with great posture—your goal here is to make your walk smooth, effortless, head-turning.
2. The next thing you need to do is to get yourself into a pair of high heels (a couple of inches to start). Heels make all the difference when you are learning to walk—and once you become graceful in your heels you'll certainly look smashing in your tennis shoes!
3. Make sure you have some time, space, and a little mellow music you like. Music always helps—if you watch models in fashion shows they match their walk to the beat. Rhythm can help you move more gracefully.
4. From the standing position, begin with the foot that's in front. Take your first step, push forward from the ball

Body Language

and toe of your back foot. Keep your steps easy, a little longer than usual but not so wide you look like you're stepping over a puddle. And make sure they're not so dainty you bob up and down. Just take a strong, confident step keeping your head up and your eyes forward.

5. Pretend there's a line on the floor and make sure the ball of each foot touches the line as you walk. (Take a few more steps and be sure your feet aren't pointing outward or inward.)

6. Keep your shoulders relaxed and let your arms swing naturally from your shoulders. Make sure your hands are relaxed. Don't grip or fidget.

A few good tips:

+ Remember, the hips "lead" the walk—they swing slightly with each step. Of course, as you get more confident, you can sway your hips a bit more and look even sexier.

+ Keep your body under your control at all times but stay relaxed.

The goal is to look smooth and graceful, not uptight.

SEATED POSES

1. This one is great for any job interview—classic. The body is slightly angled with legs uncrossed, knees together. What I love about it most is that I can feel comfortable sitting like this in a short skirt without worrying about flashing anyone.

2. Sit so your gams look great. If you cross your legs too close to the knee, the flesh of the calf will bulge from the knee pressure. The best way to sit is so that the lower legs fall parallel to each other from crossed knees. Rather than strain the top leg to meet the bottom leg-line, place the lower leg in a slight diagonal line.

How to Be Sexy

4. No full frontal! While sitting, twist slightly so that your weight is mostly resting on one side or the other, with one hip turned out. If you face the lens dead on, your legs look like they are growing out of your rib cage, and your body overall will appear wide.

THE OVER-THE-SHOULDER GLANCE

This is a personal favorite of mine, because I think of it as a secret, seductive one-two punch. Picture this: You have turned your back and are walking away at a calm, cool pace. Suddenly, you pause in your tracks, turn your head, placing chin to shoulder with a smooth whip of the neck (even more effective if your hair swings as you do it). Count to three; raise an eyebrow, look your subject up and down, or give a coy little smirk, then off you go again on your merry way. Just be warned: This can be one powerful little pose if you do it with the right amount of confidence and attitude. Men have been known to turn to Jell-O . . .

O'Hara had all those Southern gents wrapped around her little finger just with a sly smile and a "Fiddle dee-dee"? She knew exactly what she was doing.

As with any skill you learn, you need to determine which approach to seduction best fits your personality. Personally, I am a girly girl. I like a man to make the first move. I want to be swept off my feet and thrown down and kissed so hard I can't breathe. I don't like to be the one who initiates passion, but that doesn't mean I'm not actively flirting. A man might think he is doing all the work to win me over, but don't be fooled, mister: Us girls, we know what we're doing. I've never been the girl that would walk up to someone and ask him out. But I might walk by deliberately, and give him a little extra hip swivel . . . then wait for him to approach me.

Women have incredible power to seduce. We've been blessed with physical assets that drive men wild; you need to learn how to harness that power to get the attention of that cute guy at the end of the bar, before he notices the ten other women who are also trying to catch his eye. We all know that in the long run, it's what's on the inside that counts, but he's never going to get to see what an amazing person you are if you don't figure out how to get him to notice you first.

And once you've got their attention, men are not all that complex to figure out, ladies. They all come with pretty much the same set of operating instructions. What motivates them? What gets them all hot and bothered and begging for more? Three basic things:

1. The thrill of the chase. So put on your running shoes, babe, and let him eat your dust. Always leave him wanting more (even if you're already smitten).
2. Competition. There's a reason why they're all glued to football on Sundays. They love a prize fight, a contest, a war. So if there is suddenly something or someone who is competing for your attention, a guy will do his damnedest to win your affection.

3. Surprise. Boredom is a boy's worst enemy. No guy wants to feel trapped in a rut or routine or worse, the *R* word ("relationship"). Keep him on his toes and he'll be hooked. He'll always wonder what you've got up your sleeve next—and will do *anything* to find out.

Seven Steps to Surefire Seduction

There's something about him that makes your pulse pound harder. Maybe he's the next-door neighbor you've known for years who's really nice to your dog, or maybe he's just walked into your favorite watering hole and is so smokin' hot, you wonder if you should pull the fire alarm. Whatever the case, all you know is that you want to make him feel the same pulse-racing, stomach-churning excitement about you that you feel for him. These seven steps will help to make sure his heart skips a beat whenever you're around.

1. LOOK DEEP INTO MY EYES . . .

Remember when we talked about the importance of eye-contact in Chapter 2? It's not just a great way to exude confidence, it's also a killer indicator of interest. Our eyes are our most expressive feature, so when you're looking to make him sit up and take note, try these tips:

+   To get a guy to notice you in a crowded place, make fleeting eye contact with him a few times over the course of the night. Don't get all crazy stalkerish, but glance over in his direction occasionally, catch his eye, flash a coy little smile, and then look away.
+   Once he's come over to you—and he will—look him directly in the

the table at dinner? When I reached for my drink at the bar, did I let my fingers glide over yours? Surprise! These little physical maneuvers not only stimulate him just when he's least prepared, they have the ability to send an electrical pulse right through his body and up to his brain.

I love to be touchy-feely. It lets you be intimate in public places (a turn-on by itself) and it definitely gets across the point that you want to get physical sooner rather than later. My favorite touch: warm breath on the nape of the neck. Wait till he's paying the bar tab then sneak up behind him, get close, and blow. Don't be surprised if the hair on the back of his neck stands on end (or something else stands at attention). It's a very powerful move; use it with caution . . .

3. BE A LADY OF MYSTERY

As I said earlier, men prefer a challenge. This is a good thing, girls. Use it to your advantage. I know it's tempting to pour out your heart and soul on a first or second date, to tell the guy everything about you ("I wore braces for three years," "Hey, did ya know my real name is Tara?"). I am all for honesty in relationships. But sometimes, there's such a thing as too much information, you know? I don't feel the need to reveal every little detail of my personal life. Let him peel away the layers and gradually discover the real you. Leave him curious, intrigued, and aching to know more. Afraid he'll never call again? Well, if you strike his curiosity, it's guaranteed that he'll be back. You can reward his persistence with a little tantalizing tidbit: "You know, when I was in high school, my nickname was TP and it didn't stand for toilet paper . . ." Let his imagination run wild—after all, you don't have to tell him any more than that.

Another mysterious maneuver: Don't tell him everything you're doing; let him draw his own conclusions. If he thinks you have no other options out there (translation: you have no other dates on the horizon), you're suddenly not as interesting. But if you're cagey about what you've been up to— "Oh, you tried to call me last night? I must have been too busy to come to

the phone . . ."—you leave him dying to know more details. Shhhh, don't say another word. Extra points if you actually *were* doing something interesting. Next time you're waiting for him to call, go out and do something cool—catch a free performance in a local park, or check out the new sex shop in town, or add an entry to your blog.

And sound like a mysterious lady when you speak. Lower your voice into a sexy whisper or a raspy growl. Talk slowly and deliberately, roll your tongue, hush certain words and emphasize others. Try saying, "I would love to see you tonight. I am so excited," in your normal voice. Now say it like you're starring in an X-rated flick. Think Marilyn, Jackie O, Farah Fawcett, even Jessica Simpson. Be breathless. Be baby doll. Be bad, bad, bad. Give him (or part of him) a cute little nickname. You don't have to say anything nasty if it's not your style (although I do recommend giving it a try at least once). Just say it in a way that will make him weak in the knees.

4 . THE SCENT OF A WOMAN

Scent is incredibly powerful—it makes a beeline right for the brain, where it churns up an intense emotional, even sexual reaction. In fact, a study at the Smell and Taste Treatment and Research Foundation showed that certain scents—lavender, doughnuts, buttered popcorn, and pumpkin pie, among others—do cause sexual arousal in men. How? It's pretty simple (without getting into all the biological stuff). Smell evokes images in our minds. It's like an olfactory flashback. A whiff of wildflowers can take you back to a romantic picnic in the park; the smell of fresh cookies in the oven can remind you of your happy days as a child. I'm not saying that you should go dab some cinnamon buns behind your earlobes or tuck a chocolate chip cookie into your décolletage, but you can find a signature scent that makes you feel sexy—whether it's sweetly floral, passionately musky, or even yummy vanilla (the big winner in that scientific study)—and layer it on everywhere you think he might get a hint of it. Your neck, your wrists, the small of your back, behind your knees, and of course, between your breasts. Just make sure it's not too overpowering (god forbid you should smell like an NYC cab). You want to seduce him—not choke him. My fave scents are Dior Addict and Pilar and Lucy's perfumes and oils; I always dab them behind my ears and on my wrists. If you want it to be lighter, spray it in the air and walk through the cloud of scent.

5. LAUGH AT HIS JOKES

I'm serious. Guys like to think they're funny. If you get his sense of humor, chances are you will get him for the long haul. I am a giggler; I can't seem to stop laughing when I'm on a date. It actually makes you relax; it lightens things up. And most guys feel great about the fact that they are so entertaining and witty that they keep me amused. I would just caution you not to overdo it (falling off your chair in a hysterical fit of laughter is a bit much—and besides, most floors are filthy!). And try not to laugh when it's inappropriate—you want him to know you have a good sense of humor, not a nervous tic.

6. STROKE HIS . . . EGO

Go ahead, give the guy a round of applause. Tell him if he's looking buff or that you love his new tie. Focus on all his positives instead of the negatives. And don't be afraid to compliment. I just read an article by a woman who had written a book about animal trainers. She found that men respond just like animals to positive feedback, and she shared a great piece of advice: The best way to encourage a behavior you like from your man is to reward him for it. He brought you a single red rose—thank him with a passionate kiss that says, "I appreciate all you do for me—no matter how small." He held the door for you? Flash him your sexiest grin. You know how we ladies melt over a compliment? It works like a charm for men, too. There's nothing as seductive as the rush you get when someone tells you something nice. He'll feel ten feet tall—like a hero or a heartthrob. And all it takes is three little words: "You look amazing . . ."

going for the *tease* part of striptease here). If you get nervous, just re-member the five *S*'s of a successful striptease: strut, slink, shimmy, shake, *then* strip.

+ Turn your back to him occasionally, so he has a chance to appreciate all of you. Peek at him over your shoulder.

+ Dare to go as bare as you feel comfortable—even if it's just taking off your blazer to reveal a lacy camisole underneath. I promise, no matter what you take off, he'll be tantalized.

Guaranteed Ways to Turn Him Off

As long as we're discussing what to do to get a guy all worked up, we should go over what will cool things down quicker than a cold shower. Everyone screws up from time to time. You get nervous, you say or do the wrong thing, and Mr. Right turns into Mr. Not Tonight. It happens. Chances are if one little thing sends him packing, he wasn't the man of your dreams anyhow. But that said, there are certain things you should remember as seduction no-no's.

1. BRAGGING, BOASTING, AND BITCHING . . . OH, MY!

If you spend the entire evening talking about how fabulous you are—and you never let him get a word in edgewise—you can bet you'll find yourself surfing the Web on Saturday nights. Confident is great, but cocky and con-ceited are just not attractive. I have always found that people who toot their own horns too loudly are really insecure. It's all a cover-up for how inferior they feel. Would you want to be in a relationship with someone who harbors such incredible insecurity? I rest my case.

Guys love it when you ask a lot of questions—about them, mostly. They like to feel like they are the center of the universe, so try turning the conversation back in his direction now and then. Toss in an occasional, "What do you think?" and he'll be purr like a kitten. This will also give you a chance to practice your sexiest, most flirtatious "I want you *now*" look—or to finish your meal!

Another major mistake: Complaining too much. Your drink is too weak; your dinner is cold; your boss is a lunatic. Bitch, bitch, bitch, bitch, bitch. Is your life really that bad? Is the universe really aligned against you? I doubt it. No guy would like to be on the receiving end of such negativity. He's probably thinking, "God, if she's this critical of a burger what is she going to say about *me*?" So grin and bear it, baby. Chances are you're just trying to think of something to say, but it's just as easy to say something positive as to be hypercritical. If you've got to complain, save the venting for your girlfriends.

2. DON'T DISCUSS YOUR EX-FILES

Wanna scare him away? Here's the quickest way: Spend the entire evening discussing your messy breakup with your ex in all its gory detail. Sure, he says he wants to know about him—he's worried how he'll compare. But if you talk, talk, talk about your recent (or not so recent) relationship, he's going to think you're either a) still into your ex, b) rebounding, or c) such an emotional wreck, you're in no condition to date. A few words of explanation are sufficient: "Yeah, we were together three years. It's over." If he persists, tell him you're focusing on the future (with him) rather than dwelling on the past. And for god's sake, *don't* show him any pictures of the two of you together!

3. SCOPE AT YOUR OWN RISK

Okay, it's hard not to stare when a drop-dead gorgeous hunk strolls by, even when you're on a date. It's like a Pavlovian response; sometimes you just can't keep your eyes from wandering and checking people out. Hey, we're only human. But take it from me, there is no greater turn-off than sitting there across the table from someone who is eyeballing every cutie who struts by. I had a funny situation when Dave and I were first dating. We would go to Sushi-Roku all the time, almost every day. We had a great time (and great food), but I started to notice that he was constantly looking around the

room. I finally got so annoyed, I asked, "What's up? You're always checking out other girls. I understand if a pretty girl goes by . . . but this is rude!" He apologized and explained himself: "I'm almost blind—I think I know someone, but only see shapes and colors. Unless they are standing two feet in front of me, I can't be sure. So I'm just trying to see people, that's all." He had Lasik eye surgery shortly after, so of course I forgave him. But unless you're legally blind, I wouldn't advise scoping out a room in the presence of your date. He'll think you're already looking for a replacement. (Well, now what's your excuse, Dave?)

4 . TABLE THE HIGH TECH

Silence that cell phone and switch off the Sidekick. You might feel important fielding calls and text messages from your friends all night and think it makes you look popular and desirable, but he'll feel neglected and lose interest faster than you can say ring tone.

5 . SQUASH THE SQUIRMING

I am a fidgeter. My foot or my fingertips are always tapping, and if I'm standing, I tend to shift or shimmy a little. I'd like to say it's because I'm a dancer and I like to move (I hope that's what my date thinks), or that I have a lot of energy, but most likely it's because I'm a little nervous and shy sometimes. While this can be sweet and charming, you should try and keep the fidgeting under control. A person who is a chronic squirmer can be distracting on a date. I always imagine that someone who can't stand still for two seconds is going to bolt on your relationship with little provocation. Not aware if you're oversquirming? Ask a close pal to observe you once or twice in a social setting. He or she will tell you what moves you need to minimize.

6 . DON'T TURN INTO NEEDY NELLIE

The one thing any guy will tell you is an instant turn-off? A girl who is pathetically possessive, needy, and naggin'. Guys hate to feel the walls closing in

How to Be Sexy

on them. Most of them are not looking to date their mothers (well, not consciously anyway)—they don't want to answer to you or keep a curfew or explain why or when or what they're doing. If you're suddenly glued at the hip, he'll freak and run. Men need time outside of the relationship, so sweetie, give him some space. Didn't you ever hear that absence makes the heart grow fonder? I know when you're really hooked on someone, it's tempting to stalk him, call frequently, text obsessively, or show up on his doorstep 24/7—but back off and he'll come begging for more. So, go have a fun night out on your own while he's out with his boys. He'll see you don't really need him and he'll think, "Gee, this babe is a find! I can date her and still watch football every Sunday with the guys." Let him do it (at least for now). He'll appreciate your independence, and his.

ACKNOWLEDGMENTS

Many thanks to . . .

My sister, Debbi, my dad, Harry Patrick, for working several jobs in order for me to study the arts, Grandma Dolores for all her Love and Glamour and her family, Channa, Chad, and Jill, my brothers, especially my bro Mark for bringin' the rock into our house (keep drummin!), Myra, Mishelle, B-Real, Priscilla, Senen, Rosie, Daisy, and Chico, Stephanie Simon, Gregg Simon, Michael Simon, Jen Merlino, Dave Navarro, Ken Paves, Amanda Reno, Mikala, Shana, Britt Reece, Jack Ketsoyan, Jill Fritzo, Ivana, Jude Alcala, Marie Ambrosino, Mama Make-Up, Renee Farrell, Pat McGrath, Karen Mitchell, Melissa Cunningham-London, Monica Ortiz, Shane Sparks, Rod Aissa and everyone at MTV, Randee St. Nicholas, Nancy S., Adam Shankman, Dean Young, Fly Di, Tai Kimbrough, Jamie King, Carla Kama, *Playboy*, and all my dance teachers, "The House of Electra" (ha, ha!), Richard Trejo, Davey Newkirk for his sense of high fashion. We wouldn't expect anything less, Amy Norris, Sugar K, Daisy and Keiko.

All the incredible people who helped me do this book: Sheryl Berk, Becky Cole, Rex Bonomelli, Caroline Cunningham, Kimberly Nordling-Curtin, the rest of the folks at Broadway Books, Frank Weimann and The Literary Group, Robert Phipps, Jim Crawford, Jay and Cathrine Goldstein, and Sharon Camposeo.